D0325977

Making Cocoa for Kingsley Amis

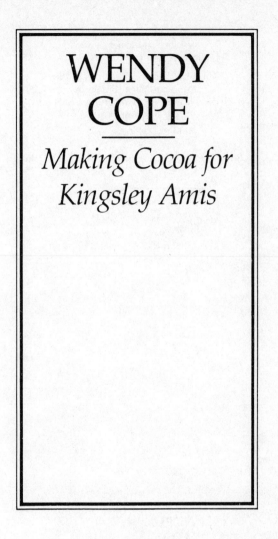

WENDY COPE

Making Cocoa for Kingsley Amis

faber and faber

LONDON · BOSTON

First published in 1986
by Faber and Faber Limited
3 Queen Square London WC1N 3AU

Filmset by Wilmaset Birkenhead Wirral
Printed in Great Britain by
Redwood Burn Ltd Trowbridge Wiltshire

© Wendy Cope 1986

British Library Cataloguing in Publication Data

Cope, Wendy
Making Cocoa for Kingsley Amis.
I. Title
821'.914   PR6053.0653/

ISBN 0–571–13977–9
ISBN 0–571–13747–4 (Pbk)

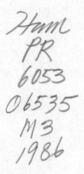

To Arthur S. Couch
and everyone else who helped

Acknowledgements

Aquarius, Bananas, London Review of Books,
New Premises (Radio 3), New Statesman, Observer,
The Pen, Poetry Book Society Supplement,
Poetry Now (Radio 3), Poetry Review,
Quarto, Rollercoaster (Radio 4), Spectator,
The Times Literary Supplement, Vogue.

Contents

I

II

III

I

Engineers' Corner

Why isn't there an Engineers' Corner in West-
minster Abbey? In Britain we've always made
more fuss of a ballad than a blueprint . . . How
many schoolchildren dream of becoming great
engineers?
                Advertisement placed in The Times *by the*
                                    Engineering Council

We make more fuss of ballads than of blueprints –
That's why so many poets end up rich,
While engineers scrape by in cheerless garrets.
Who needs a bridge or dam? Who needs a ditch?

Whereas the person who can write a sonnet
Has got it made. It's always been the way,
For everybody knows that we need poems
And everybody reads them every day.

Yes, life is hard if you choose engineering –
You're sure to need another job as well;
You'll have to plan your projects in the evenings
Instead of going out. It must be hell.

While well-heeled poets ride around in Daimlers,
You'll burn the midnight oil to earn a crust,
With no hope of a statue in the Abbey,
With no hope, even, of a modest bust.

No wonder small boys dream of writing couplets
And spurn the bike, the lorry and the train.
There's far too much encouragement for poets –
That's why this country's going down the drain.

13

All-Purpose Poem for State Occasions

The nation rejoices or mourns
As this happy or sombre day dawns.
Our eyes will be wet
As we sit round the set,
Neglecting our flowerbeds and lawns.

As Her Majesty rides past the crowd
They'll be silent or cheer very loud
But whatever they do
It's undoubtedly true
That they'll feel patriotic and proud.

In Dundee and Penzance and Ealing
We're imbued with appropriate feeling:
We're British and loyal
And love every royal
And tonight we shall drink till we're reeling.

A Policeman's Lot

The progress of any writer is marked by those moments
when he manages to outwit his own inner police system.
Ted Hughes

Oh, once I was a policeman young and merry
                                          (young and merry),
Controlling crowds and fighting petty crime
                                          (petty crime),
But now I work on matters literary (litererry)
And I am growing old before my time ('fore my time).
No, the imagination of a writer (of a writer)
Is not the sort of beat a chap would choose
                                          (chap would choose)
And they've assigned me a prolific blighter
                                          ('lific blighter) –
I'm patrolling the unconscious of Ted Hughes.

It's not the sort of beat a chap would choose
                                          (chap would choose) –
Patrolling the unconscious of Ted Hughes.

All our leave was cancelled in the lambing season
                                          (lambing season),
When bitter winter froze the drinking trough
                                          (drinking trough),
For our commander stated, with good reason
                                          (with good reason),
That that's the kind of thing that starts him off
                                          (starts him off).

15

But anything with four legs causes trouble
                              (causes trouble) –
It's worse than organizing several zoos (several zoos),
Not to mention mythic creatures in the rubble
                              (in the rubble),
Patrolling the unconscious of Ted Hughes.

It's worse than organizing several zoos (several zoos),
Patrolling the unconscious of Ted Hughes.

Although it's disagreeable and stressful
                              (bull and stressful)
Attempting to avert poetic thought ('etic thought),
I could boast of times when I have been successful
                              (been successful)
And conspiring compound epithets were caught
                              ('thets were caught).
But the poetry statistics in this sector (in this sector)
Are enough to make a copper turn to booze
                              (turn to booze)
And I do not think I'll make it to inspector (to inspector)
Patrolling the unconscious of Ted Hughes.

It's enough to make a copper turn to booze
                              (turn to booze) –
Patrolling the unconscious of Ted Hughes.

after W. S. Gilbert

16

Reading Scheme

Here is Peter. Here is Jane. They like fun.
Jane has a big doll. Peter has a ball.
Look, Jane, look! Look at the dog! See him run!

Here is Mummy. She has baked a bun.
Here is the milkman. He has come to call.
Here is Peter. Here is Jane. They like fun.

Go Peter! Go Jane! Come, milkman, come!
The milkman likes Mummy. She likes them all.
Look, Jane, look! Look at the dog! See him run!

Here are the curtains. They shut out the sun.
Let us peep! On tiptoe Jane! You are small!
Here is Peter. Here is Jane. They like fun.

I hear a car, Jane. The milkman looks glum.
Here is Daddy in his car. Daddy is tall.
Look, Jane, look! Look at the dog! See him run!

Daddy looks very cross. Has he a gun?
Up milkman! Up milkman! Over the wall!
Here is Peter. Here is Jane. They like fun.
Look, Jane, look! Look at the dog! See him run!

A Nursery Rhyme

*as it might have been written
by William Wordsworth*

The skylark and the jay sang loud and long,
The sun was calm and bright, the air was sweet,
When all at once I heard above the throng
Of jocund birds a single plaintive bleat.

And, turning, saw, as one sees in a dream,
It was a Sheep had broke the moorland peace
With his sad cry, a creature who did seem
The blackest thing that ever wore a fleece.

I walked towards him on the stony track
And, pausing for a while between two crags,
I asked him, 'Have you wool upon your back?'
Thus he bespake, 'Enough to fill three bags.'

Most courteously, in measured tones, he told
Who would receive each bag and where they dwelt;
And oft, now years have passed and I am old,
I recollect with joy that inky pelt.

A Nursery Rhyme

as it might have been written
by T. S. Eliot

Because time will not run backwards
Because time
Because time will not run
> *Hickory dickory*

In the last minute of the first hour
I saw the mouse ascend the ancient timepiece,
Claws whispering like wind in dry hyacinths.

One o'clock,
The street lamp said,
'Remark the mouse that races towards the carpet.'

And the unstilled wheel still turning
> *Hickory dickory*
> *Hickory dickory*

dock

Waste Land Limericks

I

In April one seldom feels cheerful;
Dry stones, sun and dust make me fearful;
Clairvoyantes distress me,
Commuters depress me –
Met Stetson and gave him an earful.

II

She sat on a mighty fine chair,
Sparks flew as she tidied her hair;
She asks many questions,
I make few suggestions –
Bad as Albert and Lil – what a pair!

III

The Thames runs, bones rattle, rats creep;
Tiresias fancies a peep –
A typist is laid,
A record is played –
Wei la la. After this it gets deep.

IV

A Phoenician called Phlebas forgot
About birds and his business – the lot,
Which is no surprise,
Since he'd met his demise
And been left in the ocean to rot.

V

No water. Dry rocks and dry throats,
Then thunder, a shower of quotes
From the Sanskrit and Dante.
Da. Damyata. Shantih.
I hope you'll make sense of the notes.

Triolet

I used to think all poets were Byronic –
Mad, bad and dangerous to know.
And then I met a few. Yes it's ironic –
I used to think all poets were Byronic.
They're mostly wicked as a ginless tonic
And wild as pension plans. Not long ago
I used to think all poets were Byronic –
Mad, bad and dangerous to know.

Emily Dickinson

Higgledy-piggledy
Emily Dickinson
Liked to use dashes
Instead of full stops.

Nowadays, faced with such
Idiosyncrasy,
Critics and editors
Send for the cops.

Proverbial Ballade

Fine words won't turn the icing pink;
A wild rose has no employees;
Who boils his socks will make them shrink;
Who catches cold is sure to sneeze.
Who has two legs must wash two knees;
Who breaks the egg will find the yolk;
Who locks his door will need his keys –
So say I and so say the folk.

You can't shave with a tiddlywink,
Nor make red wine from garden peas,
Nor show a blindworm how to blink,
Nor teach an old racoon Chinese.
The juiciest orange feels the squeeze;
Who spends his portion will be broke;
Who has no milk can make no cheese –
So say I and so say the folk.

He makes no blot who has no ink,
Nor gathers honey who keeps no bees.
The ship that does not float will sink;
Who'd travel far must cross the seas.
Lone wolves are seldom seen in threes;
A conker ne'er becomes an oak;
Rome wasn't built by chimpanzees –
So say I and so say the folk.

Envoi

Dear friends! If adages like these
Should seem banal, or just a joke,
Remember fish don't grow on trees –
So say I and so say the folk.

Advertisement

The lady takes *The Times* and *Vogue*,
Wears Dior dresses, Gucci shoes,
Puts fresh-cut flowers round her room
And lots of carrots in her stews.

A moss-green Volvo, morning walks,
And holidays in Guadeloupe;
Long winter evenings by the fire
With Proust and cream of carrot soup.

Raw carrots on a summer lawn,
Champagne, a Gioconda smile;
Glazed carrots in a silver dish
For Sunday lunch. They call it style.

Lonely Hearts

Can someone make my simple wish come true?
Male biker seeks female for touring fun.
Do you live in North London? Is it you?

Gay vegetarian whose friends are few,
I'm into music, Shakespeare and the sun.
Can someone make my simple wish come true?

Executive in search of something new –
Perhaps bisexual woman, arty, young.
Do you live in North London? Is it you?

Successful, straight and solvent? I am too –
Attractive Jewish lady with a son.
Can someone make my simple wish come true?

I'm Libran, inexperienced and blue –
Need slim non-smoker, under twenty-one.
Do you live in North London? Is it you?

Please write (with photo) to Box 152.
Who knows where it may lead once we've begun?
Can someone make my simple wish come true?
Do you live in North London? Is it you?

On Finding an Old Photograph

Yalding, 1912. My father
in an apple orchard, sunlight
patching his stylish bags;

three women dressed in soft,
white blouses, skirts that brush the grass;
a child with curly hair.

If they were strangers
it would calm me – half-drugged
by the atmosphere – but it does more –

eases a burden
made of all his sadness
and the things I didn't give him.

There he is, happy, and I am unborn.

Tich Miller

Tich Miller wore glasses
with elastoplast-pink frames
and had one foot three sizes larger than the other.

When they picked teams for outdoor games
she and I were always the last two
left standing by the wire-mesh fence.

We avoided one another's eyes,
stooping, perhaps, to re-tie a shoelace,
or affecting interest in the flight

of some fortunate bird, and pretended
not to hear the urgent conference:
'Have Tubby!' 'No, no, have Tich!'

Usually they chose me, the lesser dud,
and she lolloped, unselected,
to the back of the other team.

At eleven we went to different schools.
In time I learned to get my own back,
sneering at hockey-players who couldn't spell.

Tich died when she was twelve.

At 3 a.m.

the room contains no sound
except the ticking of the clock
which has begun to panic
like an insect, trapped
in an enormous box.

Books lie open on the carpet.

Somewhere else
you're sleeping
and beside you there's a woman
who is crying quietly
so you won't wake.

From June to December

1 Prelude

It wouldn't be a good idea
To let him stay.
When they knew each other better –
Not today.
But she put on her new black knickers
Anyway.

2 A Serious Person

I can tell you're a serious person
And I know from the way you talk
That what goes on inside your head
Is pure as the whitest chalk.

It's nice to meet serious people
And hear them explain their views:
Your concern for the rights of women
Is especially welcome news.

I'm sure you'd never exploit one;
I expect you'd rather be dead;
I'm thoroughly convinced of it –
Now can we go to bed?

3 Summer Villanelle

You know exactly what to do –
Your kiss, your fingers on my thigh –
I think of little else but you.

It's bliss to have a lover who,
Touching one shoulder, makes me sigh –
You know exactly what to do.

You make me happy through and through,
The way the sun lights up the sky –
I think of little else but you.

I hardly sleep – an hour or two;
I can't eat much and this is why –
You know exactly what to do.

The movie in my mind is blue –
As June runs into warm July
I think of little else but you.

But is it love? And is it true?
Who cares? This much I can't deny:
You know exactly what to do;
I think of little else but you.

4 *The Reading*

In crumpled, bardic corduroy,
The poet took the stage
And read aloud his deathless verse,
Page by deathless page.

I gazed at him as though intent
On every word he said.
From time to time I'd close my eyes
And smile and nod my head.

He may have thought his every phrase
Sent shivers down my spine.
Perhaps I helped encourage him
To read till half past nine.

Don't ask what it was all about –
I haven't got a clue.
I spent a blissful evening, lost
In carnal thoughts of you.

5 *Some People*

Some people like sex more than others –
You seem to like it a lot.
There's nothing wrong with being innocent or
high-minded
But I'm glad you're not.

6 *Going Too Far*

Cuddling the new telephone directory
After I found your name in it
Was going too far.

It's a safe bet you're not hugging a phone book,
Wherever you are.

7 *Verse for a Birthday Card*

Many happy returns and good luck.
When it comes to a present, I'm stuck.
If you weren't far away
On your own special day,
I could give you a really nice glass of lager.

8 Love Story

I thought you'd be a pushover;
I hoped I wouldn't hurt you.
I warned you this was just a fling
And one day I'd desert you.

So kindly in your spectacles,
So solid in your jacket,
So manly in your big white car
That must have cost a packet.

I grew to like you more and more –
I didn't try to hide it.
Fall in love with someone nice? –
I'd hardly ever tried it.

The course of true love didn't run
Quite the way I'd planned it.
You failed to fall in love with me –
I couldn't understand it.

9 Spring Onions

Decapitating the spring onions,
She made this mental note:
You can tell it's love, the real thing,
When you dream of slitting his throat.

10 I'll Be Nice

I'll be nice to you and smile –
It's easy for a man to win –
But I'll hate you all the while.

I shall go the extra mile
And condone your every sin –
I'll be nice to you and smile.

You will think I like your style;
You'll believe I've given in
But I'll hate you all the while.

Safe as an atomic pile,
Good as nitroglycerine,
I'll be nice to you and smile.

I'll say hypocrisy is vile
And give a reassuring grin
But I'll hate you all the while.

Set against my wits and guile,
Manly strength won't save your skin.
I'll be nice to you and smile
But I'll hate you all the while.

My Lover

For I will consider my lover, who shall remain
   nameless.

For at the age of 49 he can make the noise of five
   different kinds of lorry changing gear on a hill.

For he sometimes does this on the stairs at his place of
   work.

For he is embarrassed when people overhear him.

For he can also imitate at least three different kinds of
   train.

For these include the London tube train, the steam
   engine, and the Southern Rail electric.

For he supports Tottenham Hotspur with joyful and
   unswerving devotion.

For he abhors Arsenal, whose supporters are
   uncivilized and rough.

For he explains that Spurs are magic, whereas Arsenal
   are boring and defensive.

For I knew nothing of this six months ago, nor did I
   want to.

For now it all enchants me.

For this he performs in ten degrees.

For first he presents himself as a nice, serious, liberated
   person.

For secondly he sits through many lunches, discussing
   life and love and never mentioning football.

For thirdly he is careful not to reveal how much he
   dislikes losing an argument.

For fourthly he talks about the women in his past,
   acknowledging that some of it must have been his
   fault.

For fifthly he is so obviously reasonable that you are
  inclined to doubt this.
For sixthly he invites himself round for a drink one
  evening.
For seventhly you consume two bottles of wine between
  you.
For eighthly he stays the night.
For ninthly you cannot wait to see him again.
For tenthly he does not get in touch for several days.
For having achieved his object he turns again to his
  other interests.
For he will not miss his evening class or his choir
  practice for a woman.
For he is out nearly all the time.
For you cannot even get him on the telephone.
For he is the kind of man who has been driving women
  round the bend for generations.
For, sad to say, this thought does not bring you to your
  senses.
For he is charming.
For he is good with animals and children.
For his voice is both reassuring and sexy.
For he drives an A-registration Vauxhall Astra estate.
For he goes at 80 miles per hour on the motorways.
For when I plead with him he says, 'I'm not going any
  slower than *this*.'
For he is convinced he knows his way around better
  than anyone else on earth.
For he does not encourage suggestions from his
  passengers.
For if he ever got lost there would be hell to pay.
For he sometimes makes me sleep on the wrong side of
  my own bed.

For he cannot be bossed around.

For he has this grace, that he is happy to eat fish fingers
or Chinese takeaway or to cook the supper himself.

For he knows about my cooking and is realistic.

For he makes me smooth cocoa with bubbles on the top.

For he drinks and smokes at least as much as I do.

For he is obsessed with sex.

For he would never say it is overrated.

For he grew up before the permissive society and
remembers his adolescence.

For he does not insist it is healthy and natural, nor does
he ask me what I would like him to do.

For he has a few ideas of his own.

For he has never been able to sleep much and talks with
me late into the night.

For we wear each other out with our wakefulness.

For he makes me feel like a light-bulb that cannot switch
itself off.

For he inspires poem after poem.

For he is clean and tidy but not too concerned with his
appearance.

For he lets the barber cut his hair too short and goes
round looking like a convict for a fortnight.

For when I ask if this necklace is all right he replies,
'Yes, if no means looking at three others.'

For he was shocked when younger team-mates began
using talcum powder in the changing-room.

For his old-fashioned masculinity is the cause of
continual merriment on my part.

For this puzzles him.

Rondeau Redoublé

There are so many kinds of awful men –
One can't avoid them all. She often said
She'd never make the same mistake again:
She always made a new mistake instead.

The chinless type who made her feel ill-bred;
The practised charmer, less than charming when
He talked about the wife and kids and fled –
There are so many kinds of awful men.

The half-crazed hippy, deeply into Zen,
Whose cryptic homilies she came to dread;
The fervent youth who worshipped Tony Benn –
'One can't avoid them all,' she often said.

The ageing banker, rich and overfed,
Who held forth on the dollar and the yen –
Though there were many more mistakes ahead,
She'd never make the same mistake again.

The budding poet, scribbling in his den
Odes not to her but to his pussy, Fred;
The drunk who fell asleep at nine or ten –
She always made a new mistake instead.

And so the gambler was at least unwed
And didn't preach or sneer or wield a pen
Or hoard his wealth or take the Scotch to bed.
She'd lived and learned and lived and learned but then
There are so many kinds.

Message

Pick up the phone before it is too late
And dial my number. There's no time to spare –
Love is already turning into hate
And very soon I'll start to look elsewhere.

Good, old-fashioned men like you are rare –
You want to get to know me at a rate
That's guaranteed to drive me to despair.
Pick up the phone before it is too late.

Well, wouldn't it be nice to consummate
Our friendship while we've still got teeth and hair?
Just bear in mind that you are forty-eight
And dial my number. There's no time to spare.

Another kamikaze love affair?
No chance. This time I'll have to learn to wait
But one more day is more than I can bear –
Love is already turning into hate.

Of course, my friends say I exaggerate
And dramatize a lot. That may be fair
But it is no fun being in this state
And very soon I'll start to look elsewhere.

I know you like me but I wouldn't dare
Ring you again. Instead I'll concentrate
On sending thought-waves through the London air
And, if they reach you, please don't hesitate –
Pick up the phone.

Giving Up Smoking

There's not a Shakespeare sonnet
Or a Beethoven quartet
That's easier to like than you
Or harder to forget.

You think that 'sounds extravagant?
I haven't finished yet –
I like you more than I would like
To have a cigarette.

Manifesto

I'll work, for there's new purpose in my art –
I'll muster all my talent, all my wit
And write the poems that will win your heart.

Pierced by a rusty allegoric dart,
What can I do but make the best of it?
I'll work, for there's new purpose in my art.

You're always on my mind when we're apart –
I can't afford to daydream, so I'll sit
And write the poems that will win your heart.

I am no beauty but I'm pretty smart
And I intend to be your favourite –
I'll work, for there's new purpose in my art.

And if some bloodless literary fart
Says that it's all too personal, I'll spit
And write the poems that will win your heart.

I feel terrific now I've made a start –
I'll have another book before I quit.
I'll work, for there's new purpose in my art,
And write the poems that will win your heart.

II

Mr Strugnell

'This was Mr Strugnell's room,' she'll say,
And look down at the lumpy, single bed.
'He stayed here up until he went away
And kept his bicycle out in that shed.

'He had a job at Norwood library –
He was a quiet sort who liked to read –
Dick Francis mostly, and some poetry –
He liked John Betjeman very much indeed

'But not Pam Ayres or even Patience Strong –
He'd change the subject if I mentioned them,
Or say "It's time for me to run along –
Your taste's too highbrow for me, Mrs M."

'And up he'd go and listen to that jazz.
I don't mind telling you it was a bore –
Few things in this house have been tiresome as
The sound of his foot tapping on the floor.

'He didn't seem the sort for being free
With girls or going out and having fun.
He had a funny turn in 'sixty-three
And ran round shouting "Yippee! It's begun."

'I don't know what he meant but after that
He had a different look, much more relaxed.
Some nights he'd come in late, too tired to chat,
As if he had been somewhat overtaxed.

'And now he's gone. He said he found Tulse Hill
Too stimulating – wanted somewhere dull.
At last he's found a place that fits the bill –
Enjoying perfect boredom up in Hull.'

Budgie Finds His Voice

From The Life and Songs of the Budgie
by Jake Strugnell

God decided he was tired
Of his spinning toys.
They wobbled and grew still.

When the sun was lifted away
Like an orange lifted from a fruit-bowl

And darkness, blacker
Than an oil-slick,
Covered everything forever

And the last ear left on earth
Lay on the beach,
Deaf as a shell

And the land froze
And the seas froze

'Who's a pretty boy then?' Budgie cried.

Usquebaugh

Deft, practised, eager,
Your fingers twist the metal cap.
Late into the moth-infested night
We listen to soft scrapings
Of bottle-top on ridged glass,

The plash and glug of amber liquid
Streaming into tumblers, inches deep.
Life-water. Fire-tanged
Hard-stuff. Gallons of it,
Sipped and swigged and swallowed.

Whiskey: its terse vowels belie
The slow fuddling and mellowing,
Our guttural speech slurring
Into warm, thick blather,
The pie-eyed, slug-witted slump

Into soused oblivion –
And the awakening. I long
For pure, cold water as the pump
Creaks in the yard. A bucket
Clatters to the ground. Is agony.

The Lavatory Attendant

I counted two and seventy stenches
All well defined and several stinks!
                    Coleridge

Slumped on a chair, his body is an S
That wants to be a minus sign.

His face is overripe Wensleydale
Going blue at the edges.

In overalls of sacerdotal white
He guards a row of fonts

With lids like eye-patches. Snapped shut
They are castanets. All day he hears

Short-lived Niagaras, the clank
And gurgle of canescent cisterns.

When evening comes he sluices a thin tide
Across sand-coloured lino,

Turns Medusa on her head
And wipes the floor with her.

E Pericoloso Sporgersi

But a modulation to D flat minor
argues for pronouns of a different kind:
the consideration of history as syntax
or a slow dance of nomadic stones.
No wonder the flight of the pigeon
over the Piazza Cortina at sunset
becomes a gesture of the purest angst.

Pastruccio knew what to make of such
gratuitous moments, the refractions
of inveterate light. In a garden
of non sequiturs the silkworm dozes,
ignorant of Spinoza and unworried
by sex or the darkening obscurity
of sonorous sentences like these.

My cat piddles on the carpet and yawns.
Art, he reflects, is rivalled only
by a cargo of absolutes sailing northwards
to Goethe's incomparable parakeet.
The gods dream dictionaries and sonatinas.
Beyond the window their shadows lengthen,
aspiring to the stature of a late quartet.

Duffa Rex

I

King of the primeval avenues, the municipal parklands: architect of the Tulse Hill Poetry Group: life and soul of the perennial carousals: minstrel: philatelist: long-serving clerical officer: the friend of everyone who's anyone.

'Pack it in,' said Duffa, 'and buy me a drink.'

II

He digs for the salt-screw, buried in crepitant spud-slivers. Speaks of his boyhood in the gruntler's yarg, the unworked cork-bundles, coagulations of nurls.

The mockery of his companions is unabated. It is the king's round, they urge. His hoard is overripe for commerce.

One by one he draws coins to the light; examines them: exemplary silver, his rune stones. Treasure accrued in a sparse week, to be invested in precious liquid.

Strugnell in Liverpool

for Allen Ginsberg, Charlie Parker,
T. S. Eliot, Paul McCartney, Marcel Proust
and all the other great men who have
influenced my writing

waking early
listening to
birdsong watching
the curtains brighten
like a shirt
washed in Omo
feeling the empty
space beside me
thinking of you

crawling out of
bed searching
for my glasses
piles of clothing
on the carpet
none of it yours

alone in the toilet
with the Harpic
and the Andrex
thinking of you

eating my cornflakes
plastic flowers on
the windowsill green
formica table lovesong
on the radio bacteria
in the drainpipe
thinking of you

going
up
stairs
again
and
getting
dressed

think-
ing
of
you

thinking
of you your pink
nylon panties
and your blue
nylon bra
Body Mist
hairsmell of Silvikrin
shampoo and your white
nylon panties

thinking of you

Narrative

The sky was dark, the garden gnomes were still
When Schopenhauer observed, 'I like them less
Than sausages – in fact they make me ill.'
The vicar nodded once and murmured, 'Yes,
But wouldn't Tacitus have praised the skill
Of all those jugglers on the Leeds express?'
It seemed they had decided not to tell
The governors that Fido wasn't well.

Nijinsky's role in this remains mysterious –
We know he knitted cardigans for both
The Spanish twins and, while he was delirious,
Composed an ode to economic growth –
And yet one wonders if Chagall was serious
About the cigarette or merely loath
To recognize that others took for granted
The yellow birdbath he had always wanted.

God and The Jolly Bored Bog-Mouse

*Strugnell's entry for the Arvon/Observer
Poetry Competition 1980. The competition
was judged by Ted Hughes, Philip Larkin,
Seamus Heaney and Charles Causley.*

God tried to teach Mouse how to sing.
'Piss off! I'm not the sort.'
Mouse squelched away across the bog.
'It's jolly cold,' he thought.

Stone-numb, Mouse watched the ice-bright stars,
Decided they were boring.
Cradled in roots and sodden turf,
Soon he was jolly snoring.

Mouse dreamed a Universe of Blood,
He dreamed a shabby room,
He dreamed a dank hole in the earth,
(Back to the jolly womb).

Mouse tried to vomit up his guts
Then got up for a pee.
A comet pulsed across the sky –
He didn't jolly see.

From Strugnell's Sonnets

for D. M. Thomas

(i)

The expense of spirits is a crying shame,
So is the cost of wine. What bard today
Can live like old Khayyám? It's not the same –
A loaf and Thou and Tesco's Beaujolais.
I had this bird called Sharon, fond of gin –
Could knock back six or seven. At the price
I paid a high wage for each hour of sin
And that was why I only had her twice.
Then there was Tracy, who drank rum and Coke,
So beautiful I didn't mind at first
But love grows colder. Now some other bloke
Is subsidizing Tracy and her thirst.
I need a woman, honest and sincere,
Who'll come across on half a pint of beer.

Not from the stars do I my judgement pluck,
Although I often read my horoscope.
Today *The Standard* promises me luck
With money and with girls. One can but hope.
Astrologers may not know if you'll win
The football pools or when you'll get a screw,
But one thing's clearer than this glass of gin –
Their character analyses are true.
Cancerians are sympathetic, kind,
Intuitive, creative, sentimental,
Exceptionally shrewd and, you will find,
They make fantastic lovers, warm and gentle.
Amazing, really, that you fail to see
How very well all this applies to me.

My glass shall not persuade me I'm senescent,
Nor that it's time to curb my virile hunger.
I'm still as randy as an adolescent
And didn't have much fun when I was younger.
Pursuing girls was hopeless with my looks
(I used to pick my spots and make them worse)
So I consoled myself by reading books –
Philosophy, pornography and verse.
For years I poured my unfulfilled desire
Into sad songs – and now, to my delight,
Find women love a bard, however dire,
And overlook my paunch because I write.
One doesn't need much literary skill
To be the Casanova of Tulse Hill.

Not only marble, but the plastic toys
From cornflake packets will outlive this rhyme:
I can't immortalize you, love – our joys
Will lie unnoticed in the vault of time.
When Mrs Thatcher has been cast in bronze
And her administration is a page
In some O-level text-book, when the dons
Have analysed the story of our age,
When travel firms sell tours of outer space
And aeroplanes take off without a sound
And Tulse Hill has become a trendy place
And Upper Norwood's on the underground
Your beauty and my name will be forgotten –
My love is true, but all my verse is rotten.

How like a sprinter you have turned and run
From me, who'd loved you almost half a year.
The world's become a fridge, there is no sun,
I hardly have the stomach for a beer.
And yet I still have my guitar to strum
And books to read and some fantastic grass
That Tony got me. I sit here and hum
The tunes we used to hear in Norwood bars –
We Are All Slobs, The Muggers' greatest hit –
Do you remember? Once you said to me,
'This is their best since *Education's Shit*',
And I agreed. But I am forty-three
And blew it when I told you I'd much rather
Listen to a jazz band, like your father.

(vi)

Let me not to the marriage of true swine
Admit impediments. With his big car
He's won your heart, and you have punctured mine.
I have no spare; henceforth I'll bear the scar.
Since women are not worth the booze you buy them
I dedicate myself to Higher Things.
If men deride and sneer, I shall defy them
And soar above Tulse Hill on poet's wings –
A brother to the thrush in Brockwell Park,
Whose song, though sometimes drowned by rock
                                                                    guitars,
Outlives their din. One day I'll make my mark,
Although I'm not from Ulster or from Mars,
And when I'm published in some classy mag
You'll rue the day you scarpered in his Jag.

(vii)

At the moment, if you're seen reading poetry
in a train, the carriage empties instantly.
                    Andrew Motion in a Guardian *interview*

Indeed 'tis true. I travel here and there
On British Rail a lot. I've often said
That if you haven't got the first-class fare
You really need a book of verse instead.
Then, should you find that all the seats are taken,
Brandish your Edward Thomas, Yeats or Pound.
Your fellow-passengers, severely shaken,
Will almost all be loath to stick around.
Recent research in railway sociology
Shows it's best to read the stuff aloud:
A few choice bits from Motion's new anthology
And you'll be lonelier than any cloud.
This stratagem's a godsend to recluses
And demonstrates that poetry has its uses.

From Strugnell's *Rubáiyát*

1

Awake! for Morning on the Pitch of Night
Has whistled and has put the Stars to Flight.
The incandescent football in the East
Has brought the splendour of Tulse Hill to Light.

7

Another Pint! Come, loosen up, have Fun!
Fling off your Hang-Ups and enjoy the Sun:
Time's Spacecraft all too soon will carry you
Away – and Lo! the Countdown has begun.

11

Here with a Bag of Crisps beneath the Bough,
A Can of Beer, a Radio – and Thou
Beside me half-asleep in Brockwell Park
And Brockwell Park is Paradise enow.

12

Some Men to everlasting Bliss aspire,
Their Lives, Auditions for the heavenly Choir:
Oh, use your Credit Card and waive the Rest –
Brave Music of a distant Amplifier!

Oh, come with Strugnell – Argument's no Tonic.
One thing's certain: Life flies supersonic.
One thing's certain, Man's Evasion chronic:
The Flower that's blown can never be bionic.

51

The Moving Telex writes and having writ
Moves on; nor all thy Therapy nor Wit
Shall lure it back to cancel half a line
Nor Daz nor Bold wash out a Word of it.

Strugnell's Haiku

(i)

The cherry blossom
In my neighbour's garden – Oh!
It looks really nice.

(ii)

The leaves have fallen
And the snow has fallen and
Soon my hair also . . . . .

(iii)

November evening:
The moon is up, rooks settle,
The pubs are open.

III

Making Cocoa for Kingsley Amis

It was a dream I had last week
And some kind of record seemed vital.
I knew it wouldn't be much of a poem
But I love the title.